£1.50

First published 1974
© Copyright Joan Hodgson 1974

By the same author

HULLO SUN!
(The first book in a series
for children, of which ANGELS
AND INDIANS is the second.)

WISDOM IN THE STARS
(Esoteric astrology.)

ISBN 0 85487 033 4

Printed in Great Britain
by Fletcher & Son Ltd,
Norwich

ABOUT THIS BOOK

Joan Hodgson's 'Angels and Indians' is written for children from eight to twelve.
It is a worthy companion to her earlier book 'Hullo Sun' which has already found
a warm place in the hearts of children on both sides of the Atlantic. None knows
the child heart and mind better than Joan Hodgson, and her special gift is an ability
to put spiritual truth in a way that children of all ages love and can respond to.

Peter Ripper's splendid illustrations well match the text; and of special interest
are the photographs of fairies, the famous 'Cottingley' photographs, which for 50
years have defied all attempts to prove them other than genuine.

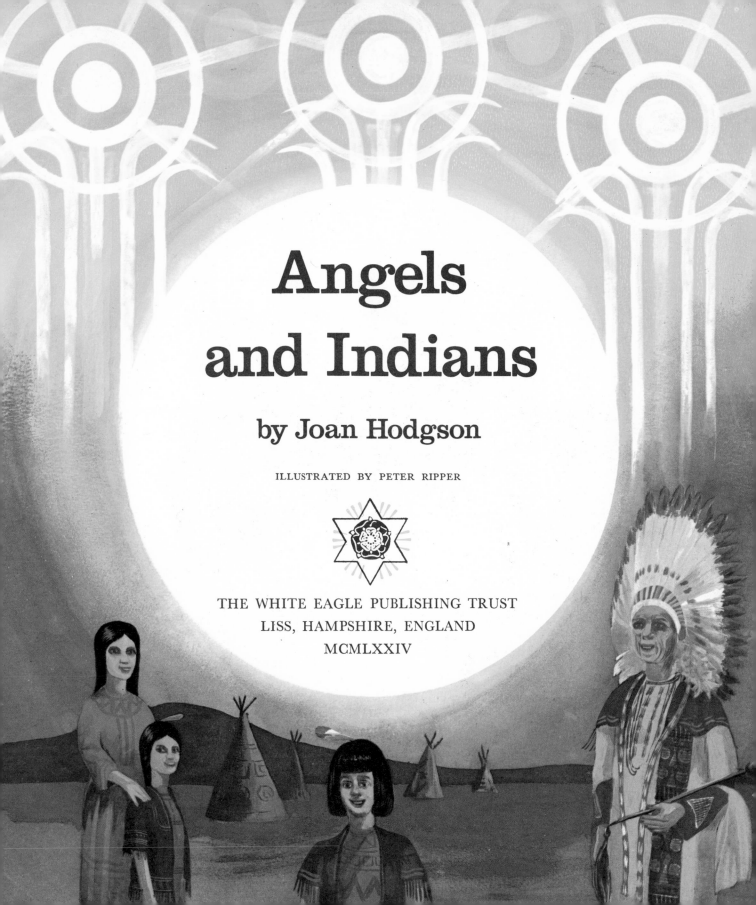

Angels
and Indians

by Joan Hodgson

ILLUSTRATED BY PETER RIPPER

THE WHITE EAGLE PUBLISHING TRUST
LISS, HAMPSHIRE, ENGLAND
MCMLXXIV

The girls who photographed fairies!

HAVE you ever seen a fairy or a gnome or a water sprite? These little nature spirits sometimes show themselves to children who are playing in the fields or woods, or in the quietest part of a garden; they are all around us wherever there are plants and trees and growing things.

Just as you have a beautiful angel, living in the world of light, who always watches over you and helps you, so all the plants and trees, all the birds, animals and insects have an angel, a fairy or a gnome who looks after their growth. All these angels and nature spirits live in the world of light. The children in the Summerland play with them and learn all about their work.

3

About this photograph and the others in this book

The full story of these photographs is told in FAIRIES: A BOOK OF REAL FAIRIES
by Edward L. Gardner, published by The Theosophical Publishing House Ltd. We are
grateful to Mr Leslie Gardner, who holds the copyright of the photographs, for his
kind permission to print them.
Readers may be interested to know that when we were discussing with our printers the
possibility of reproducing the photographs, they told us that they had printed
FAIRIES: A BOOK OF REAL FAIRIES and had in their archives the negatives from which
the prints in this book are reproduced.
Could this be more than just coincidence?

Children in earth bodies sometimes see them too, as we've already said, but usually only when they are very young or if they have what is called clairvoyance or 'second sight'; which means being able to use your inside eyes to see clearly into the world of light. Babies and very little children will see these little nature spirits without realising it, for they are still so close to the world of light from which they have come. But as you grow older and have to use your brain, and learn to read and write, and to think hard, it is as if a little door closes so that you no longer see the fairies—that is unless you train yourself to do so. This is why many people think that fairies don't exist; but what a mistake they are making!

If there are no such things as fairies, what are those little people playing and dancing round Frances in the photograph opposite?

Yes, this is a real photograph taken many years ago by Elsie, her cousin. Frances was then ten years old and was staying with Elsie who was thirteen. Elsie and her parents lived at Cottingley in Yorkshire, which was then a little country village. They lived in a cottage beside a stream, or 'beck' as they call it in Yorkshire, which tinkled alongside their garden. Elsie and Frances used to love playing in this beck. Wonderful games they would have as they paddled along, following the stream as it wound its way into a pretty glen full of trees and bushes. There they would play hide-and-seek, and when they were tired they would sit very still and watch the birds, the fish and the little creatures of the water running along the banks and darting into the beck. Most of all they liked to watch the antics of the fairies and gnomes in the beck, for both Frances and Elsie had their inner eyes open and could see clearly into the world of light. Whenever it was fine, sunny weather they would wander up into the glen. Sometimes they would take a picnic out with them and have a lovely time. Fairies and gnomes are always full of fun and pranks and the girls would try to entice them to come close and even to sit on their hands just as a little bird or wild creature might do.

At meal-times at home Frances and Elsie would chatter together about the fun they had with the fairies, and Elsie's father and mother would laugh and tease them. 'What a lot of nonsense you two are talking! You are imagining it all!' they would say.

Now, Elsie's father had a small camera. It was not like our modern cameras with cassette films which are so easy to work. Each time you took a photo you had to fit in a sensitised glass plate; then this would have to be taken out and another put in ready for the next photo. Mr Wright, Elsie's father, was quite interested in photography. He used to develop his own plates in the dark cupboard in the scullery and then take prints from them in the sunlight.

One day, after he had been teasing the two girls about their tales of the fairies, Elsie said to him, 'Look here, Father, if you'll let me have your camera and show me how it works I will try to get a photo of the fairies. We've been playing with them this morning.' Mr Wright laughed and said he wasn't going to have his plates spoiled, but the girls pleaded so hard that at last he gave in. He put one plate only in the box, and showed Elsie how to use the camera.

Off they went in great delight. Frances wasn't really so interested in the fairies as in having her own photograph taken. Almost before they had left the garden she was pestering Elsie to take it, but Elsie made her wait until they reached the part of the glen that the fairies specially liked, close to a little waterfall. If you look carefully at the picture of Frances facing page 5 you can just faintly see the splashing water on her right. The fairies soon gathered round Frances, entering into the fun as Elsie snapped them.

As soon as the picture was taken, the girls rushed back with the camera. 'I think we've got them, Father,' Elsie cried. 'Oh! please develop them quickly and let's see.' As it was a fine day Mr Wright had things he wanted to do in the garden, but he promised to develop the plate later on in the evening. The girls had to be satisfied with this promise.

The scullery cupboard where he developed the plate was very tiny, but

Elsie managed to squeeze in beside him while Frances waited eagerly outside. As soon as the plate was developed, Mr Wright was astonished to see what looked like white swans all round Frances. Elsie saw them too and called out to Frances, 'We've got them!'

In the morning they took a sun print from the plate; and the girls were delighted. Mr and Mrs Wright were utterly astonished. They didn't know what to think. They just couldn't believe that this was a real fairy picture. At first they wondered if the girls had cut out little paper figures just to tease them, although there had been no sign of any paper or scissors or drawings about the place. Mr Wright even went quietly up the glen to have a thorough search, but he could see no scraps of paper. While the girls were out playing, Mrs Wright carefully searched their bedroom but she could find no sign at all of any paper cutting. Even so, they just couldn't believe that the girls could have got a photograph of real fairies—it didn't seem possible. They questioned and questioned, but the girls assured them over and over again that this was no trick and that they really did play with the fairies up the glen.

A month later Frances and Elsie were once again allowed to take out the camera, and this time Frances took the photo of Elsie facing page 6. This was taken on a grassy bank just above the glen, and Elsie is trying to encourage the gnome to come on to her knee. Can you see his tiny pipes showing up against his wings? One of the fairies in the first picture is blowing a pipe too. Fairy folk are always full of joy and fun, and love dancing to the music of their pipes which sounds rather like trickling water but with more tune and lilt. Even today in parts of Scotland there are legends about the magic music of the fairy pipers in which of course people don't really believe; but when you see these photos you realise that the stories could be true.

Mr and Mrs Wright were really puzzled and bothered by the photographs. They couldn't believe in them and yet as both the girls had always been very truthful they couldn't believe that they were making it all up. So after taking a

few more sun prints they put them all carefully away and said no more about it; but they wouldn't let the girls have the camera again.

Frances went back home, and three years passed by. Then one day Mrs Wright went to a lecture in which the speaker talked about the work of the fairies. She then remembered the photographs which had puzzled them so much and after the lecture she went up to the speaker. She asked him if it could be true that fairies really did exist, and would it be possible that they could be photographed? She told him about the two photographs which the girls had taken in the glen, and he said he would like to see them. So Mrs Wright posted the photos to the lecturer who was most impressed and said that he would show them to his friend, a Mr Gardner, who understood more than he did about unusual photographs.

When Mr Gardner saw them he was indeed interested, and asked to see the negatives which he took to an expert on fake photography. They were put through every sort of test to try to prove that they were faked; but every expert who examined them had to admit that they were ordinary single exposures with no sign whatever of any trickery or faking. Indeed, what astonished them all was the fact that all the little figures seemed to be specially full of light and that they had actually moved during the exposure.

Mr Gardner was so impressed that he showed the pictures at a lantern lecture he was giving. They looked even better flashed up on a large screen and many people were interested and astonished. The famous Sir Arthur Conan Doyle heard about these pictures, and when he saw them he asked Mr Gardner to visit the Wright family to see if the girls could get some more photographs on specially marked plates which would give extra proof that they were genuine. If they could do so, he was going to write an article about the pictures in a famous magazine of that time.

This happened in August 1920, when Elsie was sixteen and Frances thirteen. Mr and Mrs Wright invited Frances to come and stay with them again, and the two girls were each given a beautiful new camera with a packet of specially marked plates. Unfortunately the weather did not help them. It rained and rained for almost the whole fortnight that Frances was staying in Cottingley. There were only one or two brief spells of sunshine, but in spite of this the girls managed to take three more pictures (facing pages 9, 11 and 12).

The photograph facing page 12 is specially interesting. It is called the Fairies' Sunbath, and you will see that it looks rather like a little cocoon. This is a sort of magnetic bowl made of sunlight which the fairies weave for themselves after the weather has been dull and wet. They get inside this little bowl of light to be recharged with vital force. They go in looking rather like a torch whose battery needs recharging, and come out once again sparkling with light.

All these photographs have been tested over and over again for any sign of fake. They have been enlarged with the most powerful and expensive projectors such as are used to detect forgeries, but no expert has ever been able to prove them to be anything other than simple fairy photographs. Some of the experts who have thoroughly examined them have said at last, 'Well, it looks as though I've got to believe in fairies.'

Other people have tried all sorts of ways by photographing fake fairies, just to prove that it could be done, but none of these has ever stood up to the test of the experts who can tell immediately whether a photograph is genuine.

In the olden days many people knew about the fairy world and believed in it. When Shakespeare wrote 'A Midsummer Night's Dream' and 'The Tempest', many of the audience really believed the magical parts of the play. In countries all over the world there are stories and legends of the doings of the 'little people' or the fairy folk, but nowadays most people laugh at these and do not heed them. They only believe in science and the magic which comes out of a test-tube, but nobody has yet been able to explain away these real fairy photographs taken by Frances and Elsie.

Have you got a camera? And have you ever tried to take a fairy photograph?

You never know till you try. You might be one of those people who have that special kind of magnetism in their aura which the fairies can use to make themselves visible, like Frances and Elsie had. Quite a number of such people, especially children, have the second sight or clairvoyance. They can see into the world of light which is all around us, and watch the fairies at work. Not many people have that special quality in their aura which the fairies like and which enables them to materialise enough to show up on a photograph. You never know until you try, and you may be lucky. Choose a very quiet place where you can imagine the fairies having fun and try to photograph them in a pretty, sunlit clump of flowers or by a flashing waterfall. You never know. You might get a fairy picture.

What the Indians knew

about fairies and angels

THE ancient American Indians, or, as most of us call them, the Red Indians, knew a great deal—perhaps more than any race of people has ever known—about the fairies and angels in the world of light. They lived very close to nature, to the plants and trees, to the lakes and rivers and all the little creatures who lived there, and they learned from childhood how to be very still, how to listen and to watch. The Indians in those far off days also lived close to the world of light, so were friendly with the angels of the fire, the earth, the air and the water, and knew how to work with them by obeying the spiritual laws of life. Because of this they were

15

rarely sick. If they were, they would go to the medicine man of their tribe, a wise man who knew not only how to make medicines from the plants and the bark of the trees, but also how to call upon the help of healing angels to make them well again. The medicine man taught the Indians how to keep their bodies so healthy and strong that many of them lived to a great age, yet still remained apparently young and vigorous. The young men of the tribe were in such splendid training that they thought nothing of running 125 miles in times which today would easily beat the Olympic records. You can read about this in a book called 'Gospel of the Red Man' by Ernest Thompson Seton.

These ancient American Indians worshipped God as the Great White Spirit and thought of Him as being everywhere, like the sunlight, and yet at the same time as a great and wonderful Being within the sun. They believed also that God's light shone like a little sun in their hearts, showing them what to do and how to live happily. Even as tiny children they were taught to follow the way the little light in their hearts showed them. Each morning on waking, they would stand up straight, looking towards the east, to the rising sun, and thank the Great White Spirit for the new day. With their eyes closed they would think of the sun, not the earthly sun but the Great White Spirit within the sun, and they would breathe in the light and strength which they knew that the Great Spirit was pouring down upon them. Deep in his heart the young Indian would pray,

O Great White Spirit,
Thank You for this new day.
Please help me to be kind and true
And brave all the day long,
And to do well all the work which You place before me.
May Your light shine like the sun in my heart
So that I can make the people around me
Happy.

Each evening before he lay down to rest he would look towards the west to the setting sun. Again he would breathe in the light of the Great White Spirit and thank Him for all the happy things which had happened during the day and for the ways in which He had helped him to cope with all the difficulties of the day. Quietly in his heart he would say,

O Great White Spirit,
Dear Father-Mother God,
Thank You for helping me all through the day.
Thank You for the funny things which have made me laugh,
And for the difficult things which have helped me to grow stronger.

While I sleep
Please let Your beautiful angels take me into the world of light
To have a happy time with the people I love.

In the morning may I come back to my earth body
Strengthened and refreshed
With my little light shining so brightly.

Dawn Star and Red Earth were Red Indian children who lived long ago in the days before the white men came to their country. From the time they were little papooses, as Indian babies were called, their mother helped them to use their inside eyes. Each day she would take them into the forest, showing them how to step so quietly that not even a leaf or stick crackled; showing them how to stand still as a stone, silently watching.

She taught them how to use their eyes so that they could look all round them without moving their heads even a tiny bit. When they were very still like this, the little animals and birds would peep out of their hiding-places and gradually

come out to play and frolic as if they were not there. Dawn Star and Red Earth learned how to talk to the birds and the animals and to understand their thoughts. They did this by being very still and using the little light in their hearts. In the picture on the previous page can you see how the ray of light from Dawn Star's heart is helping her to understand the little otter? Red Earth is doing the same with the bird.

Their mother would say to them, 'Now close your eyes and think of the sun. Think of the world of light which is all around us. See the body of light of the trees and flowers and the animals all around us.' Then gradually when they were still like this—the little sun inside their hearts grew very bright and helped them to see into the world of light, into a magic world. In this magic world the children began to see the nature spirits of the flowers and trees. At first it was almost more a feeling than a seeing, but gradually that inner world of light became very real.

Dawn Star specially loved the flowers and trees. She learned to know all the bushes and plants whose leaves and bark were good for making sick people well. As her little light grew bright inside her she would see clearly the fairies and gnomes playing hide-and-seek in the plants and grasses; peeping at her through the leaves; chuckling and turning somersaults to attract her attention. Do you see in the picture that these fairies and gnomes appeared to Dawn Star dressed like little Red Indians? See their gay feathers and their shining beads. Instead of pipes they are beating tom-toms for their dances. The fairy folk in the inner world always like to copy the dresses of the human people living near them.

Sometimes Dawn Star would see the angel of a tree, very tall and stately inside the trunk. Very occasionally it would come out towards her, changing form until it was rather like an Indian brave. Do you see the tree spirit in the picture? You have to look very carefully for it is in the world of light that these nature spirits live and you will see them looking rather like shafts of sunlight.

Dawn Star and Red Earth loved watching the birds and listening to their

songs. They knew where each kind of bird built its nest and all the different colours of their eggs. Often they would stand quite still in the forest and listen until gradually they could recognise the song of every bird. Red Earth, who was very good at whistling, grew clever at copying the bird songs and enticing the birds to come closer and closer. He talked to the birds in their own language through his thoughts. Red Earth found that somehow, through the little light inside him, he could talk to any animal, and it would answer him, for he would know its thoughts.

As the children listened to the birds, they also began to hear with their inner ears the music of the angels of the air as they played in the trees and ruffled the waters of the great lake near by. Sometimes they would watch these air angels building great cloud castles in the sky, and know that a big storm was coming. Then the angels of the winds would have glorious fun tossing the branches of the trees and bending them almost double as they tore along, making the water-fairies thoroughly excited and causing the salamanders, the fire spirits, to dance higher and higher until it seemed as if all the nature kingdom was in a thrilling and tumultuous dance, while the people, the animals and the birds all crept away into shelter until the storm was over.

Dawn Star and Red Earth were not afraid of storms; indeed they quite enjoyed them. Their father was the Chief of the tribe, and together with some of the other wise men of the tribe he knew well how to talk to the nature spirits and to control them if they grew too rough. These wise people knew how to quieten the spirits of the air; they knew how to call upon the angels of water to bring the rain when the ground was getting so dry that all the plants were becoming parched. They knew how to call upon the angels of the sun to bring warmth and light and happiness to the people. When they planted the corn which would feed them during the long cold winter, they prayed that the Great White Spirit would send the angels of the earth, with all their little gnomes and fairies, to help it to grow healthy and strong.

23

In the warm summer days, when they were not playing in the forest, Dawn Star and Red Earth especially loved the tumbling river which ran down into the big lake near their lodge. They would play and swim, and Red Earth especially enjoyed racing his canoe with the other boys. He was very good at this and would often win the races. The boys liked to get to the rough part of the river where the water poured down from a big fall and they would shoot the rapids.

Dawn Star did not enjoy this at all, but she loved to sit on a rock listening to the music the water made. She would open her inside eyes and watch the water sprites tumbling about, laughing in the sunlight. These little sprites could change shape very quickly. Sometimes they looked just like the fish which darted in and out among the rocks, then suddenly they were like little people, tiny Indians swimming or shooting the rapids in their canoes just as the boys were doing, and their antics would make Dawn Star laugh. Sometimes in the waterfall she would see a larger being whom she knew to be an angel of the water. This angel was quieter than the tiny sprites and more deeply hidden in the waterfall. Dawn Star had to concentrate quite hard to see this water angel, but she thought her very beautiful. Can you see the water sprites and angels in the picture?

No matter what happened in their lives, whether they were working or having fun, the Indians never forgot to think of the Great White Spirit—to thank Him and to ask for His help.

Always before eating Dawn Star and Red Earth had to be silent for a minute, saying thank you for their food and for all the things which made them happy. Then they would throw the first morsel of their food into the fire to remind them that all life comes from God, the Great Spirit behind the sun, and goes back to God.

The Indians specially loved their fires which they made from the dry wood gathered in the forest. It was the children's special work to make sure

that there was always plenty of wood in their lodge. The flames dancing and crackling among the sticks made them think of their own little light, that little flame of God in their hearts which helped them to see into the world of light.

In the evening when the sun was setting they would build a lovely fire of dry wood and pine cones. The family and their friends would gather round the fire to tell stories and sing songs. Sometimes they would just sit quietly looking into the flames and thinking of the world of light which is so close. In the stillness of the evening and the firelight they would begin to use their inside eyes to see the fire-salamanders dancing in the flames, leaping about, pulling funny faces and trying to make people laugh and feel happy. They would see too their friends and relatives (who were now living in the world of light) drawing close around them to share their happy party; to join in the laughter and the jokes; to rejoice together in the warm firelight. They were all so happy to know that they could still be together even though their loved ones no longer had an earth body.

Can you see their friends and family in the Summerland drawing close to them and sharing their fun round the fire? The people in the world of light

are not very far away and we can easily learn how to talk to them in our thoughts.

Dawn Star and Red Earth were taught how to talk to their friends in the world of light through the little light shining in their hearts. They would think of God, the Great White Spirit behind the sun, and then they would think of that light shining in their friends now living in the world of light. They would picture their friends and talk to them in their thoughts through the little light in their hearts just as they had learned how to talk to the animals and the nature spirits.

They lived so close to the angels and to the world of light that they had no fear at all of dying. They knew that when the right time came they would hear the call of the Great White Spirit and would fall asleep, leaving their earth body just as they did each night; only this time they would not have to come back in the morning. They could stay in the Summerland to enjoy a good rest and holiday until it was time to come back again as a baby, in a new body, to do some more work and learn some more lessons. We call the world of light the Summerland, because summer is a happy time when all the flowers are in bloom, but the Indians called it 'The Land of the Hereafter'.

Indians

from the

past

influence our lives today

THESE American Indian people lived a very long time ago, and perhaps you think that they can have nothing to do with your life today—but you are wrong, you know! Some of these old Indians are very busy indeed just now, for although they are living in the world of light, they know that the earth people are in very great need of their help.

For many years they have been trying in all sorts of ways to prove to us that there really is a world of light. They have brought messages from people now living in the Summerland to their friends on earth which have proved them to

be still alive, happy and busy. Perhaps it was they who helped Frances and Elsie to photograph the fairies? Most of all they are trying to teach us how to be happy and healthy like the Indians were and not at all afraid of death.

Because they know so much about working with the angels and the nature spirits, they are especially good at bringing spiritual healing to sick people, many of whom have been made better after the earthly doctors have said that this was impossible. Miracles of healing are still happening, just as when Jesus was on earth.

People living in the world of light need to work in partnership with someone in a physical body if they want to help those who are still on earth. It has to be someone who knows and understands how to use their inside eyes to see into the world of light; someone whom they love and have worked with in a previous life. Such people are called mediums, and the teacher who works with them in the world of light is called a guide. Long before they were born into their present earth body, some of these mediums knew that they were coming to earth with special and unusual work to do. Plans for this were made with their guides, many of whom were these noble American Indians. As you grow older, you may be interested to read some of the true stories about the wonderful proofs of life continuing in the world of light which these guides have brought to the earth. Some of them, such as Red Cloud, White Hawk, Silver Birch and White Eagle have become well known and loved by many people.

On the opposite page is a picture of White Eagle, the American Indian guide of Mrs Grace Cooke. There is a very interesting story about how this was painted.

Long, long ago White Eagle was a wise and beloved Indian Chief and in that life Mrs Cooke had been his daughter. Since then through many lives they have known each other and worked together to help people, and to heal those who are sick. Long before Mrs Cooke was born into this life, she and White Eagle planned to work together again, because they knew that so many people at this time were ill, unhappy and afraid of death. They planned to bring comfort, healing and sure proof that the angels really do live in the world of light, and that human people go there when they are asleep and when they leave their physical bodies at death; for this spirit world is our true home.

Of course when Mrs Cooke was born as a tiny baby she did not remember anything about the plans that she and White Eagle had made, but when she was a little girl she could see very clearly into the world of light—more so than most children do. Often she would see people who were living in the Summerland and made friends with them. She was rather a lonely little girl, for although she had a number of brothers and sisters she was very much younger than they were. Yet she did not feel too lonely because of her friends in the world of light who would talk to her and play with her.

Especially she loved a group of Red Indians who would come to see her and gather round her bed before she went to sleep at night. They would smile and talk to her and she would go off with them into the Summerland. The leader of these was very tall indeed, and wore a beautiful headdress of white feathers with blue tips. He had blue eyes which twinkled all the time with fun and laughter and she loved him very much. He told her that his name was White Eagle and that when she grew older they were going to do a lot of work together. He had his own special name for her, 'Brighteyes', because with her inside eyes she could see so clearly into the world of light. All the Indian names have a special meaning, which shows the work they have to do. White Eagle means a spiritual teacher, a priest of the sun, for the eagle is a bird which soars far above the earth into the sunlight and can see far and wide.

White Eagle promised 'Brighteyes' that one day she was going to have a picture of himself to prove to her that he was a very real person.

As 'Brighteyes' grew older she did not forget how to use her inside eyes as so many people do, but could always see clearly into the world of light. Because of her 'bright eyes' many people who were sad came to ask her if she could see

their friends who had died, and they went away happy and comforted because she had been able to tell them things which clearly proved that their loved ones were still living and happy in the world of light—things which nobody else knew about them. These people would tell their friends, who also came to talk to 'Brighteyes' and went away comforted. There were so many sad people at that time whose sons or husbands or boy friends had been killed in the wars and many of them came to see if 'Brighteyes' could bring them messages from the world of light.

As time went on 'Brighteyes' came to know White Eagle very well. Sometimes he came so close to her that she seemed to think his thoughts, and speak with his voice, a much deeper voice than her own. In fact, gradually White Eagle would take control. It was almost as if she stood on one side in the world of light while White Eagle used her voice to speak to people. This is called trance-control. White Eagle would tell people about the beautiful world of light, about their friends who were living there and what they were doing. He began to teach the earth people how they too could learn to open their inside eyes as did those ancient American Indians. He told them of the beautiful angels who can come so close to help and heal them, and he would describe to them their own beautiful guide or teacher in the world of light who was always watching for an opportunity to help them. Often he reminded 'Brighteyes' of his promise that she should have his picture. He told her that someone had already been inspired to paint it, and that he would give it to her.

Then one day a well-known artist came to see her. She had no idea who this man was, but White Eagle knew. Very soon he came so close to 'Brighteyes' that she stood aside to let him use her voice. He greeted the artist, saying that they knew each other very well, for the artist had already painted his picture. 'Oh no, White Eagle,' said the artist, 'I don't think that I have ever painted a picture of an American Indian.' 'Well,' said White Eagle, 'I think perhaps that you scarcely realised what you were doing, but you will find that you have.

If you look in one of your old portfolios of pictures you painted a long time ago, you will find two of American Indians. Mine is the one with white feathers, blue-tipped.'

When the artist went home he looked where White Eagle had told him and there in the old portfolio were the two pictures of American Indians which he had painted so many years ago and had long forgotten all about. Of course he immediately gave the picture to 'Brighteyes' who still treasures it.

All this happened quite a long while ago, and since then thousands of people have come to know White Eagle's picture and to love him, for he helps them to open their own little door into the world of light so that they can talk to their own loved ones who no longer have a physical body. He has helped them to understand that they have a lovely shining company of friends in the world of light who are always there to help and comfort them when they are ill or sad or worried.

About

White

Eagle

and the Great White Spirit

WHITE EAGLE teaches us that everybody has his own guide or helper as well as a guardian angel. Guardian angels have their own particular work to do. They have shining wings, and are different from human people. Your guardian angel watches over you to make sure that God's plan is carried out in your life; but you also have a special human friend in the world of light who can help you, through your kindest, noblest thoughts, to make your own little light bright and clear. This friend or guide knows and understands you so well. It is someone whom you have known and loved many times during your past lives on earth. Your guide may be an American Indian like White Eagle who will help you to open your eyes to the world of light or perhaps do healing work. It may be a wise man of the east, or someone who was a clever scientist, or an alchemist of the Middle Ages who understood magical secrets—a fine musician, or a kind, loving sister of mercy. According to the special work you have come to earth to do, your guide will be someone who has specialised in this kind of work during a past life and will appear to you dressed in the garments of that life.

When you are asleep at night, you often go with your own guide to one of the temples of wisdom in the Summerland where you can learn more about the things that specially interest you.

How can you get to know your own guide? How can you learn to open again the little door which will lead you into the world of light? Like Dawn Star and Red Earth, you will have to train yourself to become very quiet and still, to watch and listen and to use your imagination.

Each morning when you wake and at night before you go to sleep sit very still, tall and comfortable. Close your eyes and think of the sun. Picture it clearly, just as the Indians did; then think of God, the Great White Spirit behind the sun. Feel its light and warmth pouring down upon you, and in your heart say a prayer of thanks. You can make up your own words, or if you find it easier, learn one of the little prayers given in this book. It does not matter which. What matters is that for a few moments you think of nothing else but that beautiful Light, that Great White Spirit behind the sun, who caused you to be, and who loves and cares for you. Thank Him and worship Him in your heart. Think of the light of God shining like a little star inside you; and now breathe in that glorious light which is pouring down into your heart from the great Sun. Breathe it in gently and slowly, and as you breathe, picture your own little light growing brighter and brighter until you are just filled with light from the great sun. You feel as if you are one with the Great White Spirit. Then gently and slowly breathe out again. Do this several times until you feel as if

the little light in your heart is blazing out, radiating the light to the people around you and especially to anyone whom you know is ill or sad or worried, or to any little animal you want to help, just as Dawn Star and Red Earth sent the beam of light to their animal friends.

Now for a little while you must use your imagination. Picture the light or star in your heart growing larger and brighter, and in the centre see a little door. Open the door and go inside. Now picture yourself in such a beautiful place, the place you would most like to be. It may be a beautiful garden, or beside a little stream running through a wood, or in a sunny buttercup field; by a still pool with water lilies and with fish swimming about, or perhaps by a lovely seashore. Try to picture this place so clearly that it becomes very real to you so that you can go into it over and over again in your imagination. If you have chosen to be by the seashore, imagine you are walking on the sand. Feel the sand between your toes and smell the seaweedy scent in the air. Listen to the sound of the waves breaking on the sand. Pick up a shell and see its delicate shape and colour. Now picture the nature spirits in the water and the angels of the wind playing about you. Try to see them clearly. If you have chosen a beautiful garden, imagine it very clearly until you can really smell the scent of the flowers. Hear the murmuring bees; feel the warm sun shining upon you as you plant some seeds or bulbs. Feel the rough warm earth in your fingers. Go to a beautiful rose; touch its velvety petals and breathe in its fragrance.

You will say, 'But this is only my imagination.' Yes, so it is at first—but don't you see that imagination is a beginning. As you imagine, you build something in your thought which is like a bridge—or even a ladder into the inner world, the heaven world. Do you remember the story of Jacob's ladder?

As you make this beautiful place very real in your imagination and learn to hold it in your thoughts you really are opening the door into the inner world, the world of light. As you do this, the angels can come to you, and your own guide can come close to help you. One day, quite unexpectedly, you will find yourself seeing your own guide—seeing someone a bit older than you are who is so kind and helpful and friendly and understands just what you are longing to do. He or she may be of any nationality, with white or black, yellow or red skin, but always your guide will be kind and loving, strong and wise and will know just how to help you by popping thoughts and ideas into your head.

The first time I came to know my guide was when I was a schoolgirl, very worried by some geometry homework which just would not come out. All the evening I had worked at it, covering pages and pages of rough paper. Then suddenly I remembered what White Eagle had said about going into the inner world and asking God for help. I tore up all the used-up paper and left a clean sheet ready. I washed my hands and face and went away quietly through my little door. Looking into the sun, I asked the Great White Spirit to help me. After a little while I came back to the difficult homework. I looked—I looked again—I just couldn't believe my eyes. That geometry problem seemed so easy. All the time I had been working at it I had been missing one simple fact, which made it come out in three lines. And do you know, I was the only one in the whole class who got it right! You see, by becoming quiet and going into the inner world, I had made it possible for my guide to come close enough to pop the right idea into my mind. I had built the Jacob's ladder to heaven so that the angels and my guide could come to me. You can do this too, and you will be surprised at the help which comes when you ask in the right way. It may be just an idea popped into your mind, or you may be able to see your guide. Whatever nationality your guide takes, his or her clothes will appear to you to shine with a lovely light, and you will feel happy with him or her.

Before you leave your special place in the world of light, think again about the Great White Spirit within and behind the sun. See that light pouring down upon you. Now in that light try to picture the shining wings of the angels and the kind and loving face of Jesus, or the Buddha or whichever great teacher you specially love and reverence, smiling down at you. Try to understand that all

these wonderful teachers and healers shine like the sun because they are filled with the light of the Great White Spirit, who is sometimes called the Lord Christ or the Cosmic Christ. The Cosmic Christ is a *person* but is so much greater and more beautiful than we can possibly understand with our little human minds. We can only feel his presence shining through the great masters and teachers like Jesus, the Buddha, St Francis of Assisi or our own dear White Eagle. He shines too through your own guide and teacher and through all people who truly love God, the Great White Spirit, and who are trying to be kind, helpful and brave. All these noble people work together in the world of light, in a great shining company. They are sometimes known as 'The Shining Brotherhood' or 'The Brotherhood of the Star' for the six-pointed star is the badge which they use. Do you notice that this star is formed of two triangles, one pointing upwards and one pointing down? It helps to remind you that you have to be like the triangle pointing upwards. You have to learn to be quiet and still, and to find your own special place in the world of light. As you do this you are opening your little door, or climbing your Jacob's ladder, into the heaven world. The triangle pointing downwards reminds you that your own beautiful guide with all the shining brotherhood in the world of light will come very close to help you; and when the two triangles are joined together, you have the six-pointed star which shines so brightly, to remind you of this wonderful brotherhood of men and angels.

This six-pointed star is the symbol of the new Age of Aquarius which is just dawning—the new age of brotherhood and friendship, not only among the people on earth but between the people still in the physical world and all the angels and wonderful people in the world of light.

When you have finished your quiet time, very firmly come right back into your ordinary everyday self. Picture yourself firmly closing the little door into the world of light, and open your outside eyes. Go and make yourself busy with all the things you have to do in the outside world, but try to remember the little light shining in your heart, through which your guide and the shining brotherhood in spirit can help you.

If you try to have your quiet time each day, the world of light will gradually become very real to you and instead of having to work hard to imagine it you will really be 'there'. You will begin to know your own guide who will find all sorts of ways of proving to you that he or she really is there and helping you.

This is the real way to pray—not by saying a lot of words, but by thinking and worshipping the Great White Spirit in your heart. As you learn to do this better, your little light will grow so bright that you will become like a beautiful shining star.

The Brothers of the Star in the world of light will come so close to you, helping you when you are worried or sad, and sharing your fun and happiness. You will be able to see the jolly little fairies and gnomes and share their fun, and the angels will help you in a wonderful way to do your own special work. You will become truly happy and healthy—a brother of the Christ Star.